UNCLE JED'S BARBERSHOP

UNCLE JED'S BARBERSHOP

By Margaree King Mitchell

Illustrated By James Ransome

SCHOLASTIC INC.

New York   Toronto   London   Auckland   Sydney

ISBN 0-590-20551-X

Text copyright © 1993 by Margaree King Mitchell.
Illustrations copyright © 1993 by James Ransome.
All rights reserved.
Published by Scholastic Inc., 555 Broadway, New York, NY 10012, by
arrangement with Simon & Schuster Books for Young Readers.

12 11 10 9 8 7 6 5 4 3 2 1   4 5 6 7 8 9/9

Printed in the U.S.A.   14

First Scholastic printing, September 1994

To Kevin, who always believed in my dreams—MKM

To Gloria and Jerry Pinkney…thanks—JR

Jedediah Johnson was my granddaddy's brother. Everybody has their favorite relative. Well, Uncle Jedediah was mine.

He used to come by our house every Wednesday night with his clippers. He was the only black barber in the county. Daddy said that before Uncle Jed started cutting hair, he and Granddaddy used to have to go thirty miles to get a haircut.

After Uncle Jed cut my daddy's hair, he lathered a short brush with soap and spread it over my daddy's face and shaved him. Then he started over on my granddaddy.

I always asked Uncle Jed to cut my hair, but Mama wouldn't let him. So he would run the clippers on the back of my neck and just pretend to cut my hair. He even spread lotion on my neck. I would smell wonderful all day.

When he was done, he would pick me up and sit me in his lap and tell me about the barbershop he was going to open one day and about all the fancy equipment that would be in it. The sinks would be so shiny they sparkled, the floors so clean you could see yourself. He was going to have four barber chairs. And outside was going to be a big, tall, red-and-white barber pole. He told me he was saving up for it.

He had been saying the same things for years. Nobody believed him. People didn't have dreams like that in those days.

We lived in the South. Most people were poor. My daddy owned a few acres of land and so did a few others. But most people were sharecroppers. That meant they lived in a shack and worked somebody else's land in exchange for a share of the crop.

When I was five years old, I got sick. This particular morning, I didn't come into the kitchen while Mama was fixing breakfast. Mama and Daddy couldn't wake me up. My nightgown and the bedclothes were all wet where I had sweated.

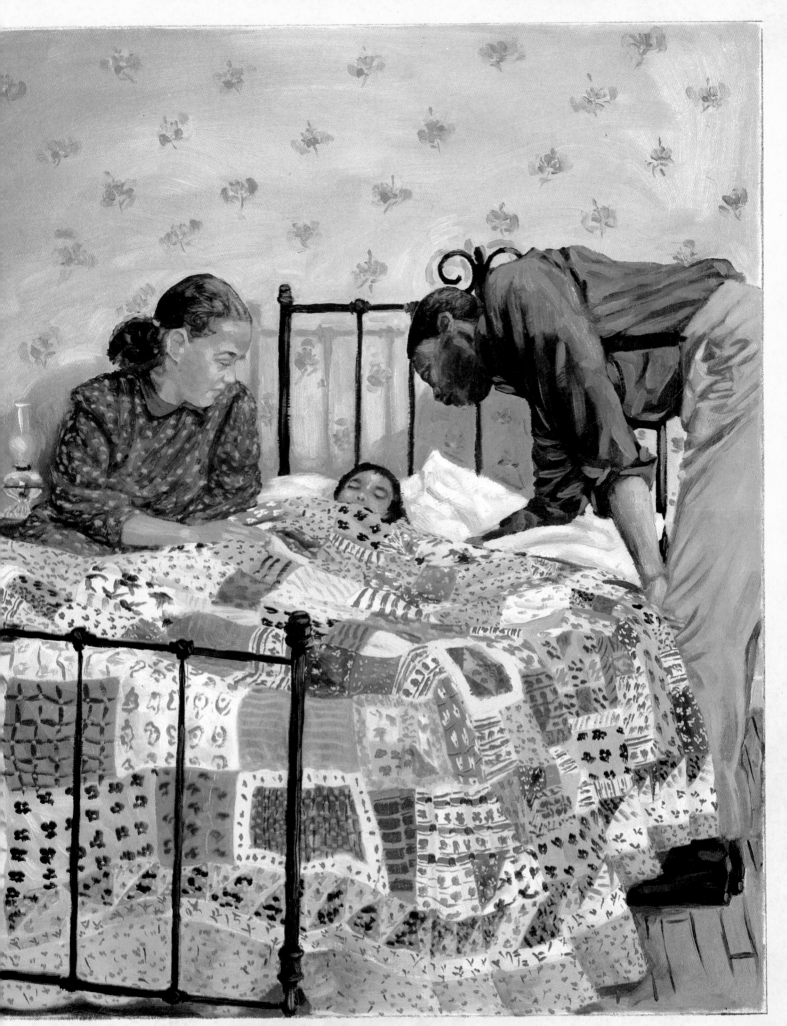

"Rochester Middle School"

Mama wrapped me in a blanket while Daddy went outside and hitched the horse to the wagon. We had to travel about twenty miles into town to the hospital. It was midday when we got there. We had to go to the colored waiting room. In those days, they kept blacks and whites separate. There were separate public rest rooms, separate water fountains, separate schools. It was called segregation. So in the hospital, we had to go to the colored waiting room.

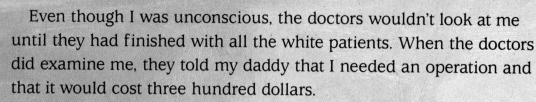

Even though I was unconscious, the doctors wouldn't look at me until they had finished with all the white patients. When the doctors did examine me, they told my daddy that I needed an operation and that it would cost three hundred dollars.

Three hundred dollars was a lot of money in those days. My daddy didn't have that kind of money. And the doctors wouldn't do the operation until they had the money.

My mama bundled me back up in the blanket and they took me home. Mama held me in her arms all night. She kept me alive until Daddy found Uncle Jed. He found him early the next morning in the next county on his way to cut somebody's hair. Daddy told him about me.

Uncle Jed leaned on his bent cane and stared straight ahead. He told Daddy that the money didn't matter. He couldn't let anything happen to his Sarah Jean.

Well, I had the operation. For a long time after that, Uncle Jed came by the house every day to see how I was doing. I know that three hundred dollars delayed him from opening the barbershop.

Uncle Jed came awfully close to opening his shop a few years after my operation. He had saved enough money to buy the land and build the building. But he still needed money for the equipment.

Anyway, Uncle Jed had come by the house. We had just finished supper when there was a knock on the door. It was Mr. Ernest Walters, a friend of Uncle Jed's. He had come by to tell Uncle Jed about the bank failing. That was where Mr. Walters and Uncle Jed had their money. Uncle Jed had over three thousand dollars in the bank, and it was gone.

Uncle Jed just stood there a long time before he said anything. Then he told Mr. Walters that even though he was disappointed, he would just have to start all over again.

Talk about some hard times. That was the beginning of the Great Depression. Nobody had much money.

But Uncle Jed kept going around to his customers cutting their hair, even though they couldn't pay him. His customers shared with him whatever they had—a hot meal, fresh eggs, vegetables from the garden. And when they were able to pay again, they did.
And Uncle Jed started saving all over again.

Ol' Uncle Jed finally got his barbershop. He opened it on his seventy-ninth birthday. It had everything, just like he said it would— big comfortable chairs, four cutting stations. You name it! The floors were so clean, they sparkled.

On opening day, people came from all over the county. They were Ol' Uncle Jed's customers. He had walked to see them for so many years. That day they all came to him.

I believe he cut hair all night and all the next day and the next night and the day after that! That man was so glad to have that shop, he didn't need any sleep.

Of course, I was there, too. I wouldn't have missed it for the world. When I sat in one of the big barber chairs, Uncle Jed patted the back of my neck with lotion like he always did. Then he twirled me round and round in the barber chair.

Uncle Jed died not long after that, and I think he died a happy man. You see, he made his dream come true even when nobody else believed in it.

He taught me to dream, too.